I Wonder Why

Pine Trees Have Needles

and Other Questions About Forests

Jackie Gaff

30254

KINGFISHER

KINGFISHER

Kingfisher Publications Plc
New Penderel House
283–288 High Holborn
London WC1V 7HZ
www.kingfisherpub.com

First published by Kingfisher Publications Plc 2005
10 9 8 7 6 5 4 3 2 1

1TR/1104/SHE/RNB(RNB)/126.6MA/F

A CIP catalogue record for this book is available
from the British Library

ISBN: 0 7534 1098 2

Series designer: David West Children's Books
Author: Jackie Gaff
Consultant: Sara Oldfield
Illustrations: Steve Caldwell 4, 5, 14–15; Chris Forsey
24–25, 28–29, 30–31; Elaine Gaffney 8, 8bl;
Neil Reed 10, 11, 12–13t, 13br, 19tr, 22tr;
Peter Wilkes (SGA) all cartoons.

Printed in Taiwan

CONTENTS

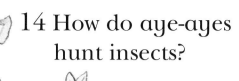

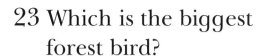

What is a forest?

A forest is a large area of land covered by trees. Beneath the trees there are smaller plants, such as bushes and flowers. Living among the plants there are all sorts of animals – insects, birds and, in some forests, bigger creatures such as foxes or wild boars.

● A single tree in an oak forest is home to as many as 400 kinds of animal, from insects and spiders to birds and squirrels.

4

How do forests help us breathe?

Like other animals, we breathe in oxygen from the air and breathe out carbon dioxide. Trees help us because they take in carbon dioxide and give off lots of oxygen.

● In a single year, a forest of 400 trees gives off enough oxygen to keep at least 20 people breathing.

Which forests have the largest trees?

The redwood forests of California, USA, have the tallest trees. Redwoods grow to over 75 metres – that's higher than a 30-storey building!

● If left unfarmed, almost any field will turn slowly into a forest. Bushes take over from grass, and then trees take over from bushes.

Where is the biggest forest?

● About a third of the earth's land is covered in forest.

Gigantic forests of conifer trees stretch right across the top of Asia, Europe and North America. The largest of these northern conifer forests is in the Russian Federation, in Asia. It makes up one-fifth of all the forest on earth.

NORTH AMERICA

● The largest rainforest is the Amazon rainforest. With an area of more than 5 million km², it covers two-thirds of South America.

SOUTH AMERICA

Tropical rainforest – mainly evergreen broadleaf trees, warm and rainy all year round.

Tropical dry forest – mainly evergreen broadleaf trees, drier than rainforest regions.

Temperate broadleaf and mixed forest – mainly deciduous broadleaf trees.

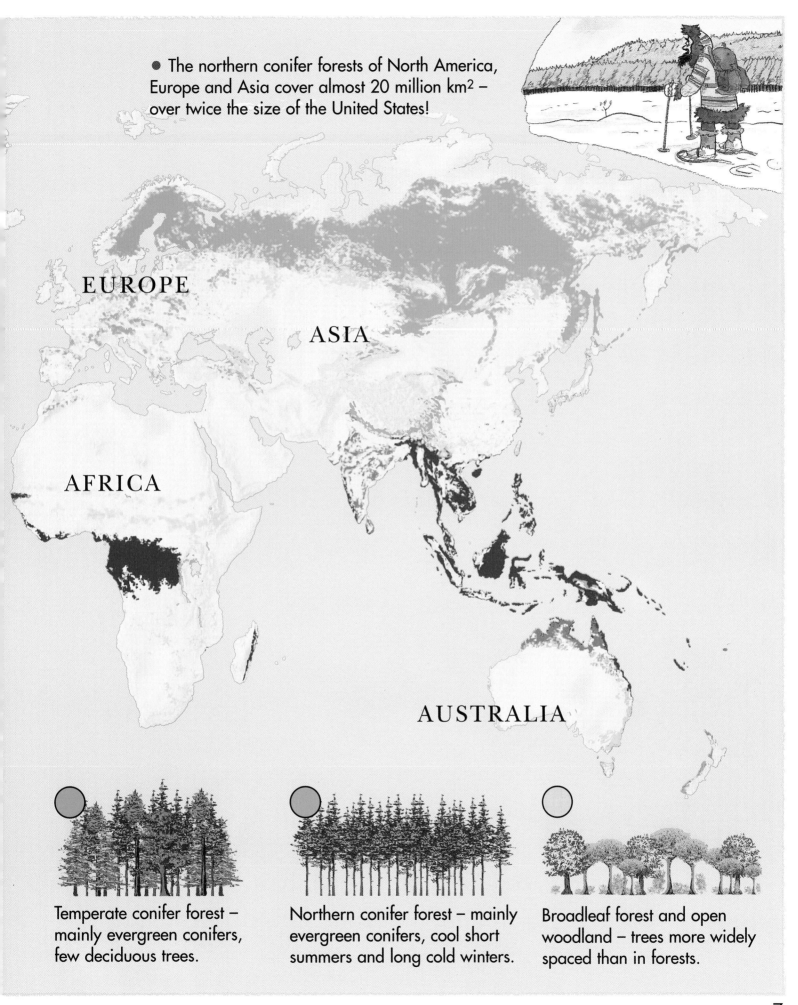

● The northern conifer forests of North America, Europe and Asia cover almost 20 million km² – over twice the size of the United States!

EUROPE

ASIA

AFRICA

AUSTRALIA

Temperate conifer forest – mainly evergreen conifers, few deciduous trees.

Northern conifer forest – mainly evergreen conifers, cool short summers and long cold winters.

Broadleaf forest and open woodland – trees more widely spaced than in forests.

What are broadleaf forests?

Sycamore

Broadleaf forests are mainly made up of broadleaf trees – maples, oaks and other kinds of tree with broad, flat leaves. The leaves of broadleaf trees come in all shapes and sizes.

Oak

Maple

Why do some forests go naked in winter?

Tree trunks and branches are woody and tough, but the leaves of most broadleaf trees are paper-thin and weak. These leaves are not tough enough to survive very cold winters. So most broadleaf trees lose their leaves in autumn, just when we start wrapping up against the cold.

● Trees that lose all their leaves in autumn are called deciduous. Trees that do not are called evergreen. Most broadleaf trees are deciduous, but not all – koalas munch on evergreen broadleafs called eucalyptus trees.

Why do pine trees have needles?

Along with cedars, firs and yews, pine trees belong to a group of trees called conifers – trees that produce cones. Like most conifers, pine trees do not shed all of their leaves in autumn. This is because the pine tree's needle-shaped leaves are small and leathery – tough enough to survive harsh winter weather.

● The smallest conifer cones are not much longer than your thumbnail. The biggest are longer than your arm!

● Crossbills are named after their oddly shaped beak. This works like a lever to help the bird get at the tasty seeds hidden inside conifer cones.

Does it rain in rainforests?

It doesn't just rain, it pours! In these tropical forests, rain tips down almost every day, and there are thunderstorms on as many as 200 days every year.

Why are rainforest trees like umbrellas?

The crowns, or tops, of rainforest trees grow so wide and thick that they act like umbrellas, stopping much of the rain from reaching the ground. They also shade out most of the sunlight, making the forest floor murky and mysterious.

● Jungles are the thickest parts of a rainforest. The plants grow so closely tangled together that the only way you can get through them is by hacking out a new path.

Emergent

Canopy

● The crowns of rainforest trees form a roof-like canopy, with a few extra-tall trees, called emergents, poking out above it.

Crown

● The crown of a rainforest tree can be as wide as a football pitch is long!

Liana

Understorey

● Giant vines called lianas scramble up the tree trunks and dangle from branches.

● The shady, lower part of the rainforest is called the understorey.

● Hidden in the gloom of the rainforest floor are millions of insects, such as army ants. These ants don't take any prisoners – they'll eat almost anything they find.

Floor

Why do plants grow in the air?

Many rainforest plants grow high up on tree branches, where they get more light than they would down on the ground. They are called air plants because their roots get the water and chemicals they need to make food from the air, not the soil.

● Some kinds of tree frog can launch themselves into the air to glide from tree to tree.

● Poison-arrow frogs are named because rainforest peoples use the poison in their brightly coloured skin as a deadly tip for arrows.

● The bee hummingbird is the world's smallest bird. It is barely 5 centimetres long.

- The hercules beetle is the world's longest. Its body is as long as a house mouse's body and tail!

Is the birdwing a bird?

No, the Queen Alexandra's birdwing is the world's biggest butterfly – named because it is bigger than many birds! It lives in rainforests in Papua New Guinea, and its outspread wings can be a whopping 30 centimetres across.

Do hummingbirds hum?

These tiny birds are named after the humming sound made by their beating wings as they hover near flowers, feeding on sugary nectar.

Why do jaguars have spotty coats?

If you have ever walked through a thick forest, you will have seen that sunlight looks spotty as it filters down through the trees. The jaguar's coat helps it hide in this kind of dappled light, ready to surprise its prey. It hunts everything from deer and wild pigs to turtles and fish.

● The jaguar is a sneaky hunter. It will dangle its tail in the water like a fishing line to attract fish.

How do aye-ayes hunt insects?

The aye-aye has an extra-long and extra-skinny finger on each hand. It uses these weird fingers to twist inside insect tunnels to hook out its favourite dinner of insect grubs. It lives in the rainforests of Madagascar, off southeast Africa.

● The aye-aye finds insect tunnels by tapping on tree trunks with its extra-long finger – and listening out for a hollow sound with its extra-big ears.

● One of the strangest-looking monkeys is the proboscis – the word means 'long, bendy nose'. Proboscis monkeys live on the island of Borneo, where they make their homes in trees near rivers.

Do spider monkeys spin webs?

No, they got their name because their long, skinny legs, arms and tail make them look a little like spiders. These monkeys are brilliant climbers and use their tail like an extra hand. They live high in the treetops in the rainforest.

● Howler monkeys are the noisiest rainforest animals. At dawn and dusk, troupes can be heard howling, to stake their claim to the part of the forest they call home.

What are cloud forests?

These beautiful, mysterious rainforests grow on the sloping sides of mountains in tropical parts of the world. Wispy clouds cling to the treetops or drift through the branches. The clouds form as warm air rises from lowland valleys into the higher, cooler mountain air.

Which tree looks like a forest?

A single banyan tree can almost turn into a forest because of its unusual way of growing. Its branches send stilt-like growths to the ground, where they take root and grow into trunks. The new trunks grow new branches, which send out more stilts. And so the banyan spreads and spreads!

● One of the biggest banyans covers an area larger than 32 tennis courts! Banyans grow in southern Asia – the record-holder is in the Botanical Gardens in Kolkata (Calcutta), India.

● The mountain gorilla lives in the cloud forests of Africa. It will often climb into the trees at night to make a cosy nest.

Where do forests grow on stilts?

Forests of mangrove trees grow in muddy water along tropical seashores. The mangrove also sends down stilt-like roots from its branches. It uses its stilts as props and anchors, not to spread itself.

● Most tree roots take oxygen from the soil, but it is hard for mangroves to do this in muddy water. Their roots take oxygen from the air instead – by sending periscope-like growths up from their stilts.

Which are the coldest forests?

Short summers and long, cold winters make the forests that grow in the far north of Asia, Europe and North America the world's coldest. Only tough trees can survive, so the northern forests are mainly made up of conifers.

● The triangular shape of conifers helps snow to slide off them.

● Wolves will eat any kind of animal, but the bigger the better. Their favourite dinner is reindeer.

Why do reindeer shovel snow?

● North American reindeer are called caribou. This is a native American word meaning 'shoveller'.

Herds of reindeer roam the northern forests. They feed on plants and other food that is hard to find when the ground is snow-covered. Their big hooves come in handy as shovels!

Where do bears go in the winter?

Bears of the northern forests escape the winter chill by snuggling up in their dens. They sleep most of the time, living off the body fat they stored up in summer.

● Raccoons also sleep through the winter in dens.

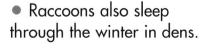

19

Which forests are always changing?

Every season brings changes to the deciduous forests and woodlands of temperate lands. Trees are bare in winter, but in spring they sprout a fresh green coat of leaves, while bluebells and other flowers carpet the ground. In autumn, leaves turn rich colours before falling.

winter   spring

What keeps foxes busy at night?

All sorts of woodland animals live nocturnal lives – awake at night and asleep in the day. Foxes come out to hunt their dinner as darkness falls. They will eat any small creatures they can catch.

● Owls hunt at night. Most have good night-time vision, but some have extra-sensitive hearing. They can pinpoint prey by the rustling noise animals make hurrying along the ground.

summer   autumn

● European badgers are also night-time creatures. Their home is an underground den called a sett and they are very house-proud. They often clean out old bedding, replacing it with a fresh supply of grass and leaves.

Do woodpeckers eat wood?

No, but they do spend most of their time pecking at it. They do this to dig out insects or to hollow out a nest.

● Muscles on the woodpecker's head act as shock absorbers, protecting its skull from the shock of drilling.

Where do koalas live?

Koalas are picky creatures. They only eat the leaves and young shoots of eucalyptus trees. So the only place koalas live in the wild is in the treetops of the Australian eucalyptus forests.

● Koalas get water from their food and rarely need to drink. Their name comes from an Australian Aboriginal word meaning 'no drink'.

● Young Australian forest animals such as possums (above) and koalas (below) start life in their mother's pouch, then hitch a cosy ride on her back.

22

● The last place you might expect to see a kangaroo is up a tree. But that is exactly where tree kangaroos spend most of their lives!

Which is the biggest forest bird?

Cassowaries are shy birds that hide in thick undergrowth in Australia and New Guinea. The largest kind can be 1.7 metres high – a s tall as some adults Cassowaries cannot fly, but they are great runners, and they can also swim.

● The kiwi of New Zealand forests cannot fly either. It is also the only bird known to have nostrils at the tip of its bill.

Who lives in the rainforests?

Tribal people get all they need from the rainforest, from food to clothes and medicines.

Many different tribes of peoples live in the world's rainforests. Most build homes in clearings and dig out vegetable plots where they grow their own food. The soil in rainforests is poor, though, without enough goodness to grow food year after year. After a few months or a few years, the rainforest people pack up and move on to another clearing.

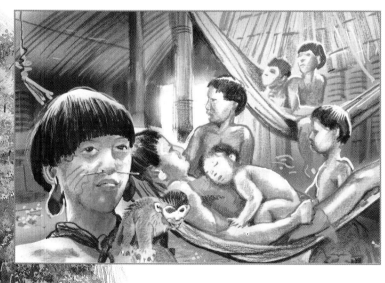

The Yanomami live in the northwest of the Amazon rainforest. Several families live together in big round houses called shabonos.

Are there schools in the rainforest?

Few tribal children go to school. Instead, their parents teach them how to survive in the rainforest – how to hunt and fish, and which plants are good to use as food or as medicine.

Do people live in northern forests?

Yes, the conifer forests of North America, Europe and Asia are home to many tribes. In Canada, for example, native Americans called the Woodlands Cree live in forest settlements.

● In northern Scandinavia, the Sami people live by fishing, hunting and herding reindeer.

25

What were the first forests like?

The first forests grew up about 350 million years ago. They were made up of tree-sized plants called horsetails and clubmosses, which looked like giant reeds and ferns.

● Huge insects lived in the first forests, including bird-sized dragonflies.

Which dinosaurs lived in conifer forests?

Conifer forests had grown up by the time of the dinosaurs. Only the larger kinds of dinosaur, such as *Iguanadon*, were tall enough to munch away on conifer leaves.

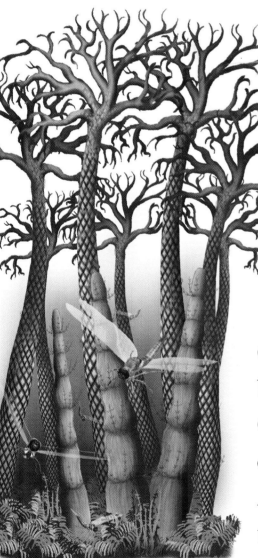

● Ancient clubmosses grew to a giant 30 metres high.

● When the plants of the prehistoric forests died, they were buried under layer upon layer of mud. For millions of years the plants were squashed and squeezed, and slowly turned into coal.

● Prehistoric insects are often found inside lumps of amber – the fossilized gum of pine trees. Fossils are the stony remains of ancient life forms.

Which tree outlived the dinosaurs?

The monkey-puzzle tree is still around today, even though it dates back to the time of the dinosaurs.

How do forests help doctors?

Forest peoples have known for a long time how to treat illness with plants, and scientists are still studying them. Eucalyptus oil is used in cough medicine, for example, while Madagascar's rosy periwinkle is used to make a drug for treating cancer.

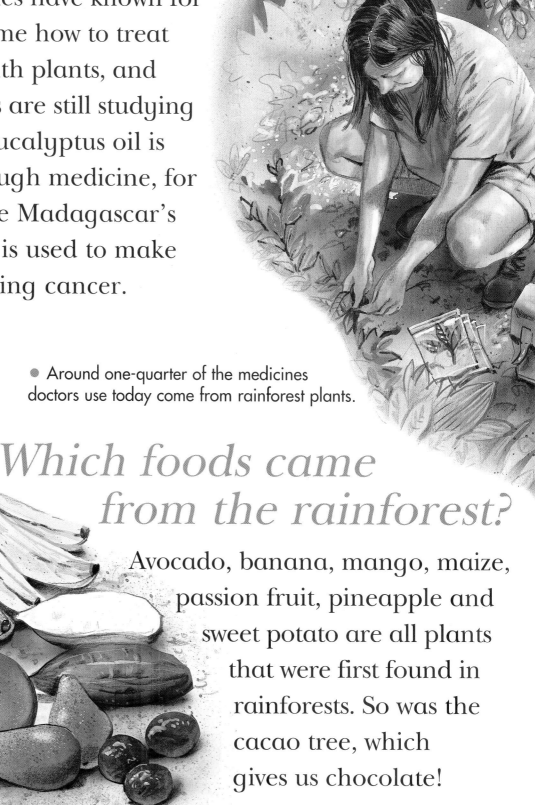

● Around one-quarter of the medicines doctors use today come from rainforest plants.

Which foods came from the rainforest?

Avocado, banana, mango, maize, passion fruit, pineapple and sweet potato are all plants that were first found in rainforests. So was the cacao tree, which gives us chocolate!

Where do chewing gum trees grow?

More than 1,000 years ago, the Maya people of Central America made a sticky discovery about a rainforest tree called the sapodilla – its milky sap makes a chewy gum. It is still used in chewing gums today.

● Rubber, made from the sap of rubber trees, was also found in the rainforests of the Americas. European explorers were amazed to see native Americans making 'shoes' by spreading the sap on their feet!

Why do people cut down trees?

Throughout history, people have cut down trees for their wood. Forests are also destroyed to clear land for farming, or for building towns and cities.

● Wood is used to make everything from furniture and houses to paper, plastics and soap.

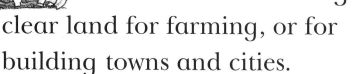

Are forests in danger?

Yes they are, because too many trees are being destroyed. Tropical rainforests are in particular danger – an area the size of England, Scotland and Wales is cut down every single year.

What are people doing to save forests?

Conservationists are people who try to protect the earth's precious plant and animal life. Together with some countries' governments, they are working to slow down the destruction of forests and plant new ones.

• The tiger is one of the many animals that are in danger of dying out because their forest homes are being destroyed.

• Some forests are set aside as national parks, where trees are protected and can't be cut down and cleared.

• Each year, 1.5 billion tree seedlings are grown in the United States. That's about five new trees for each American.

Index